Gift of Pain

Ebony D. Davis

Gift of Pain Ebony D. Davis

Copyright

© 2021 D.S.I.S Publishing. All rights reserved. No part of this book may be re-produced, distributed, or transmitted in any form or by any means, included photocopying, recording, or other electronic or mechanical methods without the prior written permission of the publisher or author. Except in the case of commercial uses permitted by copy law. For permission request write and/or email to the publisher (Ebony Davis addressed "Attention Permissions" to the email address below:

Email to:lovelyebo23@yahoo.com

Attn: Ebony Davis

Social Media: instagram @iamebonyd

ISBN: 978-0-578-85168-6

Writing Self- Publishing Consultant: Ashley Pittman www.ashleykpittman.com

To book Ebony as a speaker for your next event, please send inquiries to singlepregnantparenting@gmail.com

Website: www.iamebonyd.com

Published in The United States of America

Table of Contents

COPYRIGHT	II
TABLE OF CONTENTS	III-IV
DEDICATION	V
CHAPTER 1	1
MY PILLOW	1
CHAPTER 2	4
TOUGH	4
CHAPTER 3	13
GROWING CLOSER	13
CHAPTER 4	25
DATE NIGHT	25
CHAPTER 6	34
COME OUT COME OUT WHEREVER YOU ARE	34
CHAPTER 7	36
WHO IS SHE?	36
CHAPTER 8	38
AFTER THE STORM	38
CHAPTER 7	44
OCTOBER 22, 2015	44
CHAPTER 8	50
OCTOBER 23, 2015 (FRIDAY) DAY	50
CHAPTER 9	63
FLOATING ON EARTH	63
CHAPTER 10	66
TURNING POINT	66

CHAPTER 11:	**71**
NOVEMBER 4, 2015	71
CHAPTER 12	**74**
NOVEMBER 5, 2015	74
CHAPTER 13	**80**
DREAMS DO COME TRUE	80
CHAPTER 14	**83**
DADDY'S HOME	83
CHAPTER 15	**86**
SOCIAL MEDIA EXPOSED MY REALITY	86
CHAPTER 16	**94**
HE LOVES ME HE LOVES ME NOT	94
CHAPTER 17	**97**
BEGGING FOR MERCY	97
CHAPTER 18	**101**
THAT'S YOUR BABY	101
CHAPTER 19	**105**
I CALLED HIM JEREMIAH	105
CHAPTER 20	**109**
DELIVERANCE THROUGH FORGIVENESS	109
CHAPTER 21	**112**
CHASING AFTER HEALING	112
CHAPTER 22	**117**
"I AM"	117

Dedication

I want to dedicate this book to my Son who has completely transformed my life and perspective. I would like to dedicate this book to my sister(s), family, friends who never judged me, gave me space and allowed me to grow during this process. I want to give honor and praise to Jesus. He was the one who carried me no matter the time of day or night. I want to acknowledge and admire all the single and pregnant mothers. I know it was not an easy decision to decide to keep your child knowing you would be on this journey without the father. But, I want to encourage you through my story, that it is all working together for your good.

Chapter 1
My Pillow

It's 5:00AM Monday morning. I woke up with tears dried up on my face from the night before, just staring at the ceiling, in a dark room, with a million thoughts running through my head. I look over to my left and I see baby wipes, diapers, bottles, piled up in the closet waiting for baby's arrival. I began to scan the room once again and noticed not only the darkness, but the silence and the stillness. After 5 minutes of being awake, reality hit me again, I WAS ALONE. There was no one else here to help prepare for the baby's arrival.

I closed my eyes once more and tears began to fall slowly, hitting the pillow and leaving small but, noticeable tear stains. The alarm clock began to sound, at this time it is 6:20AM. I wiped the tears from my eyes, sat up, put both feet on the floor and proceeded to the shower to get ready for work.

I turned the shower on, and submerged my head under the warm shower, hoping to gain some type of stress relief. But, it didn't help. The longer I stayed in the shower, the more emotional I became.

I began to loudly, cry out to my father in heaven, "Father!" "Why?" Why is this happening to me?" How is it that I came so far in life, waited to have children and this is my child's story begin and end! "Father in Deuteronomy 31:6 your word says you will never leave nor forsake us." You lied to me Lord, You broke your promise. You gave me this baby without a Father! What did my unborn do to deserve this? I am sobbing; tears were flowing as heavy as the water was falling from the shower. I pounded on the wall, angrily. I was angry with myself, angry with God, and despised my child's father. Where was he during this time that I felt we really needed him? God, what? God who? Who is he? Where is he? I began to question his ability and presence.

Hmmm. I was once told by a wise man, that life can only be lived backwards. So, let us start at the beginning.

Chapter 2
Tough

On a beautiful summer day in July of 2013, I decided to visit one of my closest friends, D. The way the universe works, sometimes can be very comical. You see, I became knowledgeable of D's existence while attending high school. I have to be absolutely 100% honest, I was not a fan of hers… at all. In my opinion, she was extremely loud, joaned on people all the time, and well…. just not my speed. I avoided her at all cost. You see, I was more of a bookworm, studious, involved in extracurricular activities, quiet, easy going, minded my business type of gal. We were totally opposite of one another.

Fast forward, years later, D and I was reunited by fate at a job in 2011. She asked me a question and I irritatingly thought to myself, "Why is this girl talking to me?"! Nevertheless, we had one conversation which led to two conversations. One day while at work, D performed one of the most selfless acts a person could perform. While we were at work one day, I mentioned I was starving. She only had a few dollars. She took her last few dollars and bought us both a Nacho Bell Grande which was $1.99 at that time. That's when I knew she was genuine and true. Needless to say, D and I have been friends ever since. I didn't have a clue that she would be the link to a huge milestone in my life.

During this one particular day, D and I left her mother's house, early evening. D and I were in the middle of a conversation discussing what she was planning to cook for dinner while walking to her car. As we were discussing meal plans, she slowly backed out of her Mother's drive way and headed north down the street. As she is driving, I am gazing ahead at a young man standing a few houses down. He was leaning on the fence. From a distance, I could see his profile and mymymy he was a sight to see. He was tall, golden brown skinned, slim, with deep waves in his hair. I quickly and intensely became excited at his appearance from a distance. In my mind, I am saying to myself "who is that? "As my friend D. continued to get close to this golden brown, young, tall, man, I was able to gain a better up close and personal view of him. He was amazingly stunning in my eyes. He had beautiful, pearly white perfect teeth, gold teeth that were positioned perfectly within his set of teeth. The way he wore a white t-shirt and basketball shorts looked as if he was wearing a $200 - $300 designer outfit! Who is this well put together man that I am looking at? I thought to myself.

Screech. The car stops. D. stopped and held a conversation with this man who I had been drooling over from afar. She greeted him by saying, "Hi best friend." In return, he said "what's up best friend." I whispered to her and said. "Wait, do you know him? "She turned to me and said,

"Yes" This is my best friend Tough" Tough, this is my friend Ebony. I replied. "Hi, Tough you are cute" He replied you are too." His voice put the icing on the cake. I was so turned on! D. bluntly interrupted and said "aw naw don't start ya sh**. I just smiled and laughed. Honestly, my mind was made up, when I realized the car had stopped I knew I had to make my move.

I was always told, "Closed mouths don't get fed." I love to eat; therefore, I wasn't going to miss out on this meal. I wanted him. I had to have him. He was on my radar and I was going in for the gusto.

Reflection: what attracted you to your child's father? Who was around at the time when you met?

_____

_____

_____

_____

As we were leaving the neighborhood, Tough shouted out his phone number to D. As my hands were sweating and my heart was fluttering, I hurriedly tried to write his phone number down. HA! It was just my luck he was talking too fast and the pen wasn't working. I threw the pen and my heart flipped upside down. I felt I was being pranked. Come out now Ashton Kutcher, the jokes over.

I was extremely disappointed. I was thinking how the heck am I supposed to get in contact with him now? Well, to my surprise, D. was able to capture his number. I asked her to tell him that I wanted to take him on a date to Ruth Chris. She didn't waste any time. She immediately dialed his number and told him. He said, "Ok when?" She gave me his number and I was able to send a few text messages, before my phone abruptly stopped working.

I am screaming to myself "why, why, why!" I truly believed I would never ever see or hear from this man whom I had instantly fallen for the moment we greeted each other. However, one thing Tough and I had in common was D. and we loved her cooking. D. and her meal for the day connected the dots for us. Cha-ching!!!! Jackpot!

He called D. and asked, "What was she cooking, and could he have a plate?" D. who is extremely generous, without hesitation agreed and said "Yes." She looked at me and asked "do you want to take Tough's food to him?" I was so excited! I began to smile ear to ear. It is a wonder if she couldn't see hearts in my eyes or the cloud I was floating on. I eagerly replied, "Yes". I took Tough's food that was prepared by our friend D, from that moment on, we became inseparable.

Now, some people may suggest or wholeheartedly believe I was acting thirsty." I say, I knew what I wanted. Oh and believe I was going to get it.

Tough and Ebony sitting in the tree, k-i-s-s-i-n-g, first comes love, then come marriage, here comes Ebony with the baby carriage. HAHAHA. Yep he made me feel like a school kid with a crush the instant I locked eyes with him. If you are asking or wondering...of course, I saw and planned our whole future in 60 seconds. Tough is his name.

Chapter 3
Growing Closer

Good morning beautiful. Good morning handsome. This is the way Tough and I greeted each other every morning. It was a zealous, breathtaking feeling to wake up and hear his voice or see his message float across my screen. It was such a joy to be in his presence. Tough possesses a very fun, laid back cool cat personality. Tough could be described as being the best of both worlds. He has that pretty boy, "I am fresh and clean swag on one hand and the other hand he has that "I dare you try me" bad boy persona. My type of guy!! Tough always presented himself to look and smell like a million bucks.

The more quality time we spent together, the more I learned of him. He became increasingly attractive and irresistible. Needless to say, not only did he look and smell good. He had a great personality. He was truly the whole package.

Tough and I began to routinely go on dates, and stay overnight at each other's houses. I had trusted Tough with every bone in my body, every thought of my mind and every piece of my soul. So much so, he broke the record and earned a key to my apartment within the first few months.

We helped each other in every way we could. We shared nights of just pillow talking and getting each other's insight and opinions. I was so sure about our relationship that I even broke a rule of mine. I started cooking for him. If it was something I couldn't cook, I would take extra measures and have my sister or grandmother cook for him and pretend it was me. HAHAA. (Side note- I don't like cooking- so if I cook for you- it means you are special). Tough was special. As time progressed, we adopted royal nicknames for each other. …. The time shared between Tough and I began to pass. We began to fall deeper for each other. I can say this, because we often had conversations about our feelings.

At the time of dating Tough, I didn't have any children. He had a baby girl who was a toddler at the time. On the onset of Tough and I dating, we discussed if he wanted more kids. He told me he wanted a son eventually. I listened to him and would start imagining him being a Father to a son. We didn't talk about having additional children together. We just simply enjoyed each other and his baby girl.

Baby, I'm about to pull up, please be ready. I said to Tough on the phone. "Yep." Don't yep me you know I hate that, I replied. Tough started laughing. As I arrive at Tough's house, he is making his way down the porch to my car. Hey baby, how are you? How is your day? It's aight. Tough Replied. Tough and I began to engage in small talk as we headed to the Indianapolis Pro Basketball Game... Tough and I had a great time at the game. I actually saw a different side of him,

I had never seen before. Tough showed that he could be a little jealous. It was hilarious but cute and made me feel secure at the same time. The basketball game came to an end. We said our goodbyes to my sister and brother in law and we headed back to his house.

Queen, yes babe, I replied. I was wondering, are you ready to be a Mother? I said uhmmm, I don't know. I would -love to have a great father for my child for me to willingly have a baby. He said, I want you to have my son, can you give me a boy?" A son? I replied. Well, I haven't thought about it. But, of course I will." At that moment, we no longer used protection and we tried to have a baby.

My life with Tough was great. He and I never argued. We discussed any issues we had. We worked as a team. We complemented each other. He was my Jay z. I was his B (without the money and the fame). I would lay in bed next to him at night, say my prayers, thanking God for such a grand experience with the man of my dreams. I would whisper in his ear and say I can do this forever with you over and over and over again. I would then fall asleep wrapped in his strong arms.

As Tough and I grew closer we began to discuss financial struggles, goals and dreams in depth. Tough revealed to me that he always wanted to be a truck driver. I thought this was an awesome idea. Therefore, I took the initiative to try to get him into truck driving school. We went through the process of getting him accepted! It was an exciting moment. Oh was he ecstatic! I was happy because he was happy! But, then the advisor called back and said he can attend school, he just can't use financial aid until his felony has been seven years old. Ughhhh! There we go; the first step towards accomplishing his goal had quickly slipped right through his fingers.

Tough began to have moments when he felt like he just didn't have enough money. He would apply for jobs every day and wasn't getting too far. I could feel his energy and a deep sadness would come over me. At this time, he was the most important man in my life, so I thought it was my responsibility to make sure he was comfortable.

I continued to search for jobs that would be suitable for Tough. It was taking time to find a job that would accept felons and pay him for his experience. In the meantime, Tough started to plant a seed in my head that involved him investing in a controlled substance to make quick money. I told him he has the right and freedom to do what he wants. But, I don't date men who partake in distributing illegal controlled substances. He said he didn't want to lose me. He left the thought of distributing illegal substances alone. So, I thought.

A few weeks later, we had a heart to heart conversation regarding his financial struggles and goals. He assured and convinced me that he would be responsible, operate his controlled substance hustle at a certain time of the day and females would not be an issue. His argument was convincing. Therefore, I agreed to stay with him. The only issue was Tough didn't have the funds to put into the investment. Shocker right?

One day, as we were leaving the bowling alley, I advised Tough to pull over to the ATM bank machine. I stepped out of the car, walked over to the ATM bank machine and withdrew $800.00. I returned to the vehicle and put the crispy green dollars in his hands and told him "take off!" i.e- use this as investment towards your hustle" Omg... What was I saying? What was I thinking? Was I that stuck on stupid that not only did I agree to not leave him while he hustles, but I gave him the money to get started! I quickly discovered what the power of good looks, charm and good intimacy will do to you.

Tough began his business venture and he was earning quite well. It was appealing and attractive to see this man, I had fallen for instantaneously increase his earnings daily without any real effort. Soon after that, I found an employer who hired felons and he could drive a truck. I set up the interview. Tough showed up and he got the job! At this point, everything was adding up. All things were working in our favor. But, every now and then "Tough" would mention how his ex-girlfriend was trying to come back around by calling his sister, sparking up a conversation with him at church. I would say hmm, ok, how do you feel about it? Do you want to be back with her? He said nah I'm coo. She broke up with me because she said I work too much. I replied "Ok" I just want you to be happy." He said I am very happy. I smiled, he smiled, we smiled together.

In my head, I was thinking can this man be any more perfect? Can my life be any more perfect? After the brief conversation about his ex-girlfriend coming around, I was still confident in our relationship. I knew we were meant to be together. We were liked by friends and family. Tough eventually let his fatherly, protective guard down and allowed me to meet his daughter. That's when I was for certain this thing was real. Tough and I just made sense. We complimented each other in every way. We were both hard working, outgoing, easy going, easy on the eyes, enjoy music, fashion, motivate each other, there for each other, didn't argue, he dated me, oh and our intimacy was intense, passionate, fierce, enjoyable, emotional, romantic, and freaky all at the same time. I mean we were legitimately a power couple. Well, in my eyes we were perfect for each other and we were building a foundation for us................ and our future.

Chapter 4
Date night

Over the next month or so, the life filled with joy, laughter and abundance started to come to a halt between Tough and I. He grew distant. His conversations became short. There were moments when he just didn't answer his phone. The times I was able to contact him via phone, of course I would question, "Where has he been", what is going on? I exclaimed I could see and feel the change. As I stated previously, we did not argue. It was normal for us to have adult conversations. However, during this time, Tough became irritated. He would slightly raise his voice and then shut down! Boom, the conversation was dead and over. We would never re-visit his offbeat actions that he was presenting.

I was blinded by the mere presence of Tough, that I only saw what I wanted to see. I deliberately and boldly ignored my female intuition. Although things were taking a turn in a different direction, I kept telling myself he wouldn't lie to me; he is not a liar. He is just working. He is tired. He is a single father. He just needs space to get his thoughts and finances together. These unreal thoughts made me feel better and helped me to sleep at night.

Ring! Hello! Good morning queen! Said Tough. "Good morning King." I replied. We engaged in small talk. By the end of the call, we had made plans to go on a carriage ride and walk on the canal downtown later that evening. As we ended the call, I was smiling so hard, my cheeks started burning! Tough's voice alone would cause me to drift in a fairy tale land full of flowers, roses and strawberries. He made me feel extra warm and fuzzy inside.

I had three more hours before I could leave the workplace. The time was moving so slow, I felt as if I had gone back in time. As the clock struck 4:30pm, I eagerly exited the building and sped off in my car leaving black marks in the parking lot. I wanted to spend a little extra time grooming and dressing myself before I saw the love of my life.

The moment had arrived. It was time to go on our date. I called Tough…... no answer. I sent Tough a text….. No reply. I called again with no answer. I texted again and no reply. …Needless to say. Yep you guessed it. He stood me up!

As a woman, who was well acquainted with what the streets bring, I googled the County Sheriff's Department website; just to be sure he wasn't booked in the County Jail. If he was, that was any easy fix. I was most definitely going to bail him out. No search found, came across the screen. I sat on the couch disappointed that I had not heard from Tough. I said aloud trying to convince myself, "It's still early, its only 11:00pm, Tough will be calling soon." One tear began to fall. But I hurriedly wiped it away. I asked myself, "What are you tearing up for? The phone will ring soon.

Little did I know this was the beginning of many more tears to be shed from the infamous man nicknamed "Tough" whom I called King. At this moment, I felt like a little girl who lost her dog. I fell asleep with tears in my eyes, wondering how something that was built on a solid foundation began to crumble. I was completely clueless……

The following morning, I woke up to the birds chirping, sun shining, landscapers mowing the grass. Normally, this would be music to my ear. I would immediately become excited, ready to start my day. But, this morning was different. The sounds were not appeasing, it was just noise. I quickly picked up my cell phone to see if I had received a text, missed call, or voicemail. To my surprise, whomp, whomp in my Charlie brown voice. Nope, nada, nothing, zilch.

5. Gangsta E

F this S*** I am going to get to the bottom of this. I wiped my face off, hit the hot spots on my body with soap and water. I scanned the closet for something quick to wear. I was always taught when you are on some Bull$***, dress in all black. I got dressed in black Levi shorts, high low black shirt and black kicks. I grabbed my purse, keys, roll of quarters, sun glasses and hit the streets.

I was headed to the East side to find Tough. But, before I popped up and wasted gas. I thought it would be a better idea to call first. But, I knew I couldn't call from my phone. In my experience people don't have any issues with answering an unknown number; he/she wants to know who is calling. Therefore, I stopped at the gas station, a block from my house to use the payphone. I pulled out my roll of quarters and inserted them one by one into the slot all the while my hand is shaking and my heart is beating.

"Hello" was Tough voice on the other end. As calmly and as sweet as I could sound, I said "Hey you good?" He said "Yeah." I said, we missed our date last night, let's grab breakfast." He said, "Naw, I can't." I said, "Why?" The sweet innocent voiced, turned bitter and cold. I said, "It's coo, I am on the way. He said, "don't come over here, if you come over here I will never talk to you again." I slammed the phone, put the car in drive, and floored the gas from the North side of town to the East side. What did I have to lose, he already stood me up. I just had to see what was keeping him from me.

I arrived to the East side of town within 15 minutes. I took the back way, hoping I didn't see D. Because, I felt she would try to stop me. She saw me driving down the street and she flagged me down. Ayyyyyee E, where are you going? I just looked at her. She said, that girl down there." E, don't go down there by yourself. With a smile, I drove off and stopped at his house.

Tough's auntie was outside sweeping the sidewalk. I asked, is Tough in there? "She said, "Yes you want me to get him. Does he know you are coming?" I said "yes he does." Two minutes later, she came back to the door and said, "He isn't here." I just laughed and said. "Ok thank you." Tough and his ex-girlfriend's car was parked in front of the house. I knew he was in there. But, I wasn't giving up that easy. I wanted him to face me and be held accountable for his actions.

Chapter 6
Come out Come out wherever you are

I drove off, went to the gas station, filled up my gas tank, grabbed some snacks, and staked out three houses down from where he lived. I wasn't leaving until he came out the house. I had processed in my mind; he had to leave at least once that day. An hour had passed; I was minding my own business, keeping my eyes glued to his house while observing all activity going in and out. While I was watching his house, he had friends who were watching me. Hahahaha. One thing I can say about the hood is they do stick together.

One of his friends nicknamed Car, knocked on my window and said "run me to the gas station to get a swisher." I said, "No." He walked away. He came back moments later, asking me to do something else. I said. "Look, I know you are talking to Tough. I know you have told him, I am outside waiting on him. Since you want to deliver information, please tell him this, I have a full tank of gas, food, phone fully charged, no kids and I am off of work for three days. I am not going anywhere, until he comes out the house. Car said, "da####. Ok, my fault. I closed my car door and resumed eating my hot chips, drinking red flavored pop and staking out……

Chapter 7
Who is she?

After another hour had passed, I noticed someone was walking out of Tough's house. It was a female. She was light skinned, short in height, on the thicker side in weight, short blonde hair, with a nose ring. I said to myself that has to be his ex-girlfriend C.C. I pulled up next to the car on the driver side that the female was sitting in. She was sitting in the passenger seat with the window down. "Excuse me, is your name CC? " She said, yes why? I asked again, what's going on between you and Tough?" She said, nothing, we are just friends. I said oh ok, because I was just here and he was acting a bit strange. I was on my way to park the car, so that I could finish this conversation. I looked up and noticed Tough decided to finally come out the house. Tough, what is up? What is going on? Tough" I asked, Tough replied shamelessly "Man shaking his head while looking down at the ground. CC started to feel herself when Tough came outside. She said, "Tough" you got drama. I don't have time for that. You need to fix this." They both got in the car and drove off.

So, that was it. Tough got off scot-free. He didn't have to explain anything to either one of us. I watched them drive away in the wind. I was left sitting there in my car, with the feeling of agony, pain, and my heart in a million pieces…..

Gift of Pain Ebony D. Davis

Chapter 8
After the Storm

I had been through heartbreak before with my first love. Therefore, I was familiar with the emotions that were to follow. One minute I was up, the next I was down. one minute saying f*** him. The next minute I was saying, "how did this happen?" I experienced a spiral of emotions for the next week or so.

Surprisingly, one day as I was getting my day started, I heard, "You are my everything, everything, everything, it's all because of you I'm never sad and blue, you brighten up my day,", It stopped, and then the Mary J. Blige begin to sing the chorus once more. I walked into the room to look at my phone, it was Tough calling. I didn't expect to hear from him ever again. Clearly he made his decision and I was coming to grips with it.

I pushed ignore. "Tuh he got the nerve to be calling me." "You are my everything" Mary started singing once more. I picked up the phone and hung up. He called once more I picked up and hung up. I became angry all over again, just reminiscing on how things played out the day after he stood me up.

Over the next three weeks, Tough continued to call. I continued to ignore him. One day, I answered and said, "Whhhhaaatttttt do you want!" He said, "You." I said, "no you don't" He said, I was just going to keep calling, hoping one day, you would answer." I was silent. He said, "Can I take you to lunch on my lunchbreak? " I said, No" He said, "Please." I said "yeah." One thing about me is, I rarely turn down a meal.

I met him at a Mexican Oriental spot off of Ritter. He explained, how he was sorry, he didn't mean for that to happen, he loved me, he didn't want to lose me, could I forgive him. I was still angry, so I responded boy "No". Why are we here? He said, "I miss you." Tough and I were so into each other , that even when we were mad, we still discussed any issues, arguing was just not for us. After we finished lunch, he walked me to the car, gave me a hug and asked if he could call me. I just nodded my head.

It was so hard to stay mad at him. Tough was charming, kind, protective, handsome, and knew how to conduct himself in the rightful manner at all times. He had a way of calming me down.

Fast forward a month or so later, Tough and I had started communicating again on the regular. Our bond became closer, because not only did we have a history of being intimate, and romantic towards each other, our friendship was growing. Tough and I would just sit in front of his grandma's house, eat, talk, laugh, joke with each other, hug and kiss each other. Tough began to start asking me to come visit him at lunch while he was at work. I would go eat lunch with Tough at least once a week every week. He was working nights. He would take his lunch when I arrived. Again, we would eat, talk, laugh, joke, hug, and kiss. He would always tell me how I would make his day. He liked that he could talk to me about anything and I didn't judge him. So, here we were again, getting closer, growing, vibing, loving on each other. Maybe this time around, it will be different. I thought maybe he had his act together. Nothing can break us this time. We locked in! I would just smile every time I see him. He was my boo thang

October 22, 2015

"You are the one that I think about always. You are the one that I dream about always. My love is your love, your love is mine." It was fall Thursday evening Oct 22, 2015. I was cooking and cleaning, listening to Rihanna, you are da one. I was sipping on some Moscato and enjoying the peace. Ring...Hello... "What are you doing Queen?" Hey "King" cooking and cleaning. What are you doing? "Now you know you can't cook" Tough laughed. "I said, watch it now, yes I can". Hahaha. But, what's going on handsome, you good? He said, yes, I just want to see you. I said oh ok, where are you at? He replied work; can you come spend some time on my lunch? I said, of course. I'm on the way. I freshened up, got dressed and headed to the West side of town to his place of employment. I was full of excitement when I would see him walk across the parking lot to my car. It was never a dull moment with us. It seemed as if our souls were connected even stronger every encounter we had. It didn't matter if it was 2 minutes, or 2 days. After his lunch time was over, he would leave me with a see you later, I love you kiss that was heaven sent.

An hour later as I was preparing to go to bed, Tough called me and asked "Queen, can you come out tonight?" I said "of course." He said "I want you to come to the bar M. Event with me tonight with some of my friends from work." I said "ok, anything for you"…

Tough didn't have to beg me for too much of anything. I knew that he knew that he had me right where he wanted me. I was more than ok with that. I am a strong believer in serving a man who is deserving.

I arrived at the bar M. Event located on the West side of town. I walked into the bar, looked over to my right and there his fine, tall, skinny self was, holding the pool stick. He looked up at me and smiled and said what up "Queen? " and proceeded with a tight, warm hug and a quick soft kiss. I grabbed a stool, and placed it right in front of Tough, so I could get the full view of him. Ok babe, who is winning? I said. "Who do you think? He replied with a grin. Tough was great at any sport he played. He was great at Basketball, bowling, shooting pool, and boxing. Hahhaaha, I replied", silly me babe, I know you are the best.

"What are yall drinking" one of his co-workers interrupted. We placed our drinks order and continued to vibe. Tough, his co-workers and I stayed at the bar M. Event until 2:45am. By, this time I was nice and buzzed. Yes, we did close the bar down! HAHAHA. As I grabbed my personal belongings to walk out the door, Tough followed me. Tough is extremely protective. He wanted to make sure I was safe getting to my car. Tough walked me to my car, hugging me from behind, thanking me for spending time with him the majority of the day. You know any moment I have with you. I cherish it. I replied.

Tough asked me to get in his red truck with him for a little bit to talk. I agreed with no hesitation. Tough and I laughed, talked. In the middle of my sentence, Tough put his hand on the back of my head, pulled me close and gave me a long passionate kiss. It was the type of kiss that gave me a fluttery sensation all over my body or like I was floating on Jupiter or Mars eating donuts and ice cream without a care in the world. Hmmmm. Hmmm we said in unison as we unlocked our lips and slowly drifted apart. Good night King, Good night Queen. I hopped out of Tough's truck, opened my car door and got in.

Tough drove off and went left. I drove off and went right. We had the perfect lunch date and the perfect kick back outing. As I am driving, I drift into lala land, while listening to SWV who is an all-girl group on repeat on the CD player. I get so weak in the knees. I can hardly speak. I lose all control and something takes over me. In a daze and it's so amazing. It's not a phase. I want you to stay with me by my side. I swallow my pride. Your love is so sweet. It knocks me right off of my feet. Can't explain why your loving makes me weak.

Chapter 8
October 23, 2015 (Friday) Day

"Good morning best friend, how are you?" Kiki stated as she came into my cubicle at work. Kiki is my best friend. She stands about 4'11, shapely, nicely built, brown skinned, beautiful white pearly teeth, free spirit, nonjudgmental, and has a heart of gold. "Best friend, I am good, tired and hung over". Hahaha. Oh shoot, "best friend what did you do last night?" Kiki asked. "I hung out with Tough. It was a cool night. I really enjoyed it". "Did ya do it?" Kiki said. Hahahaha. Girl, naw. We just ate lunch together and then later on in the evening, I met him and his co-workers at the bar M. Event. I had good food, good drinks, laughter, and a little touchy feely. Aww okk best friend, "so what are you all doing this weekend?" Kiki asked. "Well as far as I know, nothing. Hopefully nothing. I am going home to go to sleep. Hahaha" Kiki, left my cubicle and we both continued to work.

Three hours later, it was time for me to clock out from work. I was so excited. I couldn't wait to get home. I was so exhausted from the night before. "Bye everyone, enjoy your weekend." I hurriedly and enthusiastically ran out of the building to my car. As soon as I opened the car door, I could feel my phone vibrate in my bag. Ughh! "Who is this"? I thought. I grabbed the phone out of my purse. I read the caller ID and discovered it was Tough calling.

Hey queen? Tough stated. Hey King, how are you? I'm coo. I was calling to see if you wanted to hang out with Kaliyah and me today? "I said, uhm, yes, sure, when? Well, in an hour or so. I am going to pick her up from school and then take her to the mall." Tough said. I replied, "Ok, cool, I'll meet you out East." He said; "yes meet me at my grandmothers." I agreed.

I was soooo tired. But, when you love someone, you sacrifice things for them. My happiness became his happiness. As long as he was happy, I was also. As far as Tough and I had come and how we have rebuilt our foundation, yep

I can truly say my love for him had come back and it was more infectious and deeper than before. I didn't have any children at this time, so it was an honor to spend time with Kaliyah and him.

I lived 10 minutes from my job. So, I decided to stop by my home for no more than 30 minutes. I wanted to change clothes, twist my curls out in my hair a little bit, and brush my teeth. As I am getting dressed, I crank the stereo up loud. I had to wake myself up. "You aint never had s***, swerve on em." Rapped Lil Boosie. Instead of getting dressed, I stood in front of the mirror, practicing my dance moves to the chorus, "swerve left, and right." Needless, to say, an hour had passed by and I was still out North swerving in the living room hahaha.

As I am putting on my left cowboy boot, I received a text. "Queen, just meet me at the mall." I said to myself, "Let me get out of here, before the night is over." I replied, "Ok handsome, I am on the way." I can't wait to see you. "Aight, I'll more than likely be inside the shoe store." He replied.

I arrived at the mall. My heart was beating, and stomach was rippling with exciting emotions. The closer I had gotten to the shoe store where Tough was at, I became anxious, hot and bothered. I effortlessly fell in love every time I seen this man. Being with Tough, never got old and to see him spend time with his daughter, turned me on even more. He was an astounding Father! I said it once and I said it again, I would love this man to be the father of my child, even if we didn't make it as a couple, I was confident he would still be a great father. I knew this, because he was not in a relationship with Kaliyah's Mother, and from what I could see, he co-parented at a tolerable level. He loved his baby girl.

I saw Tough standing with his back towards me, looking at the display of shoes in front of him. I slowly approached him and gently rubbed his arms and said "Hey babe." Tough, turned around, bent down and gave me a hug. Tough stood about six feet tall, give or take an inch. I stood 5'4 inches. So, it was perfect. Hi, Kaliyah. Kaliyah waved at me and said Hi.

Kaliyah makes a shoe selection. I overheard Kaliyah say, we should get these shoes for my little sister but Tough said not today.

So let me back it up real quick to fill in the gap of history. Cici and Tough had created a baby girl together a few months after he was confronted in the neighborhood during the period of he and I disconnection. I found out through the grapevine. He finally admitted one day, that he did have a baby girl with Cici. He also stated that he would only stay with her for the baby. He really wasn't interested in being with her. I responded, you made that bed so you have to lay in it. He said please tell me you will still be the mother of my son. HAHAHA. Boy, please. You don't even deserve my conversation, let alone, intimacy or a baby from me. Plus, I will be going off to law school in January to New York. I can't afford any distractions. Tough said, "New York?" Why? You might as well, stay here with people you know.

I was angry for a week or so. But, as you can see, I got over it. Even though, it hurt me to know the truth of him having a second baby, the reality was we were not together, when his second baby girl was conceived. To be honest, I would love the second baby girl as much as I loved Kaliyah if I had the chance. That is just how much love I had for him.

Tough wasn't the type of person to gossip or give much detail, if it didn't concern the individual. That was another quality I liked about him. My secrets were safe with him. Thus, he never really gave me any details on him and CiCi. I didn't ask any questions. I just assumed with all the constant communication, public affection and our outings, we were stepping into our new beginning.

<u>Reflect: Based on what you just read, can you pinpoint any signs that I should have left? In this reading, did you notice a reciprocated give and take or was one doing most of the giving and or</u>

taking? In this reading, is the foundation as solid as Ebony thinks?

Identifying events, circumstances, that could have led to abandoned pregnancy, and an exit

Tough, Kaliyah and I walked out of the shoe store and we explored the mall a little bit more. Kaliyah and I rode on these little character bikes around the mall. We had so much fun. I am a true kid at heart. Tough spotted some cologne, oils he wanted. Of course, I brought them for him. Seriously, the only thing he had to do was look at an item, and it was his. Hahaha. From Queen Ebony. He was spoiled.

Tough later decided he wanted to treat Kaliyah to the movies. We proceeded to

M.Donald's for a late lunch and went to the movie theater. Tough sat in-between Kaliyah and I. He held my hand tight, and rubbed them softly with light fine strokes. He exhaled and said ahhhh this feels so good. I have my Queen and my Princess with me. I looked over and kissed him on the forehead. It was good to know our feelings were mutual.

Tough and I enjoyed going on dates to the movies. In the past, it had become a tradition of ours to go to the movie theater when a newly released movie came out.

The last scene of the movie had played. The lights came on, credits were moving across the screen and people were leaving the movie theater.

Our night had finally come to an end. We had spent the entire day together and it was so peaceful, calm and pleasant.

Tough, Kaliyah and I followed the crowd outside of the movie theater to the parking lot. I helped Kaliyah get in the car and we said our goodbyes. I shut the door and began to converse with Tough. "What are you about to do Queen"? Tough asked. "I am on my way to the bowling alley. I planned to meet some friends up there." I replied. Tough leaned up against his truck and said," I just wish I could spend the whole night with you, just you and I." I just laughed and said I am a woman of my word. "I can't cancel on my people. You have had me for two days sir, and we are not even in a relationship" he asked once more. Man, "can you spend the rest of the night with me?" as he was hugging and caressing my back. "Please!" "Ok. Dang. I got you."

How could I say no? He was looking good, smelling good, touching all the right spots and he said please. I thought to myself. "Queen, follow me to drop Kaliyah off on Mitthoeffer and then to drop my truck off, I'll just hop in with you." I said ok babe… Tough got in his truck and drove off and I followed.

Chapter 9

Floating on Earth

It's Friday Night– Oct., 27 2015 8:30pm. It's a beautiful, clear, fall night. The temperature was perfect. There were stars in the sky and I couldn't imagine being with anyone else. I have my friend, lover, and homie back and he is all mine. I was saying to myself. I was always told, if you love something let it go, if it comes back, then you know it's real. I pinched myself, an yep this was really happening.

"Aye F***boy. I am about to pull up. Tough said to his cousin Vayne over the phone. He wanted to get some smoke before we made any other moves. We made a pit stop over to his cousin's house and proceeded to the drive in.

We arrived at the drive in. The movie had started. As I stated before, Tough and I didn't really talk much during movies because we didn't want to miss anything. But, this time was different. We conversed a whole lot, shooting the sh**, joking, laughing during the movie. Tough began to rub on my legs and kiss all on me. Wait a minute, I was not expecting this. Tough and I have not been intimately involved in several months. I thought. I was trying so hard to resist him, but I couldn't help it. Tough's gentle but strong touch had taken over my thoughts and my body. I had begun to lose all control. Tough whispered in my ear, "I miss you and I love you so much." I was at a loss for words. I literally felt like I had lost my voice. Nevertheless, that is all I needed to hear, I leaned back and allowed nature to take its course.

I know, I know, I know. People may wonder why you all would go to the drive in when you all just left the movies. I asked myself the same thing, and two weeks later, I discovered my life was about to drastically change!

Chapter 10
Turning Point

You are too old to have made this mistake. Girl, what are you going to do? He is already showing that he can care less? I hate this for you. Girl, this is going to be extremely hard for you. What are you going to do about Law School? A distant friend was beating these words, negative affirmations into my subconscious soul. The sensitive, self-pity, hard critic twin of my Gemini zodiac was taking it all in. I was fighting back tears as her words rang loudly in my ears because I knew the truth, but I wanted to hide it from everyone else.

As she was talking, I screamed Ahhhhhhhhhhhhhh. Ok I hear you! At this moment my heart is racing and my voice is trembling. Do you think I don't know this? Do you think I planned this? Heck, I am supposed to leave for Law school in a few months. You are absolutely right, I waited my whole life to take this step and I have to face facts that I will be doing this alone. I do not need your reminder, your statistics or your pity! I do not know how I am going to make it, but I am. I grabbed my keys and purse, stomped from the living room to the front door, and slammed the door behind me.

I cried to my heavenly Father again, weeping helplessly. Heavenly Father, I am not fit for this. I am not built for this. Please tell me why you chose me. Alone, Father, alone. Me. Why? I cried all the way home, feeling immensely overwhelmed, felt like I was drowning in guilt, pain, shame and there was no way out of this vicious hole I had dug. I was crying so hard that my false lashes began to peel off. This was the one time I didn't care if I had the lashes on or off. I had bigger fish to fry.

At the beginning of this book, I provided the back-story and history of Tough and I. However, I will now bring you into the next chapter, to what I call The Turning Point.

Dang, Eb your chest is getting big. Commented my close friend, Banks. Banks, I have a big chest anyway, so what are you talking about? I am just saying Eb, they look bigger. Ok Banks. After Banks made that comment, it made me look down and reflect back on me noticing that my bras were getting small and I had been experiencing some soreness. I guess they are a little bit bigger, but I have gained about 5 pounds. I thought to myself. Hold on, did I just add something up? ….Weight gains plus a bigger chest plus soreness. Uh oh. Could it be? Could I be with child? I said aloud. It was a thought for about 5 minutes, and then I quickly dismissed it. Because, Shortly after Tough and I shared an intimate weekend, I realized I 'couldn't continue to be emotionally, mentally, physically connected if building a future together was not in the plans. I for dang sure wasn't going to have a child by him. Therefore, I broke it off for good. I had begun to prepare to leave all behind, attend law school in New York City, find my soulmate and then -bear children. Surely, I wasn't pregnant by him. I'm just getting thicker. Who doesn't want a thick woman? I laughed to myself as I continued to beat the streets of Indianapolis up embracing the compliment Banks gave me.

Chapter 11:
November 4, 2015

Hey sister, what are you doing? You should come over; the boys are gone with their grandmother. Texted my elder sister, I replied. Ok, see ya soon. My sister and I who share the same Mother and Father, both raised by our Grandmother, both grew up at a young age were close. We had similar experiences in life and were chasing some of the same goals and dreams.

Upon my arrival, my elder sister accompanied me to the kitchen, where we usually meet just to talk and catch up on things. As we were catching up, I stopped and asked her if she had something to sip on, I.E Liquor. My brother-in-law came in the kitchen and opened the refrigerator and said, we have wine and 99 bananas. My sister and I agreed to partake in drinking 99 Bananas. I have to say I enjoyed being single and having the freedom to do whatever I pleased. I hung out with my elder sister and brother-in-law until later in the night. I left her home which is on the East side town around midnight and headed home to the North side.

I pulled up in my apartment complex around 12:30am, stepped out the car and walked into my 1 bedroom apartment. The moment, I stepped into the living room, my stomach got sick and I found myself running to the bathroom. Bluhhhhhhhh. I vomited all over the floor, walls, myself, everything and everywhere but the toilet. I dropped to the floor and sent a text message to my sister immediately.

Sister, I just threw up. My sister replied, are you serious? Do you have the stomach virus? I said "no" I don't think so. Something was strange. This sickness felt different than a stomach virus, different than a normal alcohol hang over. It was a feeling I had never felt before, But, I didn't know what it was.

I took a shower, brushed my teeth and called it a night. I fell asleep with unsettling thoughts. I was still disturbed by what had taken place.

Chapter 12
November 5, 2015

The next morning, I woke up craving grapes. I did what any person would do to satisfy a craving. I grabbed two handfuls of grapes out of the refrigerator, rinsed them, placed them in a bowl, sat on the couch and devoured the grapes like the last Supper. It was about 30 minutes later, I started feeling nauseous again. Bluh, Bluh, I ran to the bathroom…Bluh, Bluh there I went again. I vomited everywhere but in the toilet.

I just laid on the bathroom floor, feeling sick and helpless. It was 10 minutes later Bluhhhhhh, it happened again. I called my sister, she called my grandmother on three way and they diagnosed me with bearing child. My sister demanded that I purchase a pregnancy test to confirm. I agreed.

November 7, 2015

(The lines never lie)

I can't find anything to wear! Huhh! My morning was already starting off rough. I woke up late for work, I couldn't fit any work t-shirts, all of the buttons kept popping, and I couldn't stop throwing up. I was truly experiencing pregnancy symptoms from what I discovered on Google. But, I was still in denial. I was looking forward to turning up and partying the following weekend. But most of all, I WAS SINGLEEEE. Tough and I were not in a committed relationship, and if I were pregnant, how the heck would I tell him. Many thoughts ran through my mind as I drove to work in silence. Would he believe I am pregnant by him? Or would he be the typical young ignorant guy and say "it's not HIS?

I was extremely anxious all day. I wanted to know the truth. I wanted to face my fear and remove the …what if's, maybe, maybe not So, instead of eating on my lunch break, I drove to the drug store and purchased a Clear Blue Pregnancy test. My intentions were to take the test on my lunch break. But, I changed my mind, I wanted to be in the comfort of my own home. Any other day that I am working, the time moves slow as molasses. But, this particular day, it seems within the blink of an eye, it was time to clock out. So, I cleaned up my desk, finished my last task and headed out for the day. As I walked to my car, I just kept thinking this test will say negative and I can move on, pretend this scare never happened. I would then stop satisfying my fleshly desires physically while I am single. i.e abstain from sex.

I finally arrived home, changed my clothes and proceeded to the bathroom. I read the instructions on the box to make sure I was taking the test correctly and didn't receive any false results. After, I took the test; I laid it down on the tub, and walked in the kitchen. I was sweating bullets. But, I was still confident that the test would display negative results. Noppee. I was wrong. I was indeed pregnant and Tough was the

Father. I sat on the bathroom toilet, staring at the pregnancy test speechless.

(....Identifying mental and emotional feelings when discovering pregnancy

Reflection:

When you received your positive pregnancy result; what emotions did you feel? How did you think the result would change your life? Were you ready financially, mentally, emotionally?

_____

_____

_____

Chapter 13
Dreams do come true

November 8- As I stated previously, I had so many thoughts running through my head about being pregnant by someone I was no longer in a relationship with. I couldn't decide if it was best to spill the tea to Tough or save the tea for myself. I pondered 24-hours or so and I finally struck up the nerves to dial his phone number. "Hello", Tough said answering the phone. "Hello", I replied. And then, there was an awkward moment of silence. I knew who I was calling and I knew why, but the words would not come out my mouth. It seemed as if FEAR had grown arms and hands and held my mouth shut. After 30 seconds of awkward silence,

I said hey. He said, hey Queen. So, uhm, yeah, would you be upset if something came out of that weekend we spent together?" I said. He replied, noooo. Why? Did something come out of that weekend? I paused again for another 30 seconds. Studdering, y-y-yeess. Uhm, I'm pre-g-nant. For real, Tough asked. I said yes. He asked, can I come see you tonight? I said, I guess so. Yes, Sure. I would love that.

I sat on the couch with the biggest grin on my face, still holding the phone. I couldn't believe it. He wasn't upset. As a matter of fact, he wants to come over. Yesssss. Jackpot! Everything will be just perfect. Dreams do come true! Our child will share the DNA of two admirable, hardworking, loving, caring individuals. I could not wait until 10pm. I was anxious to see the Father of my unborn child.

Chapter 14
Daddy's Home

Knock Knock! Who is it? I asked, Queen open the door. I hurriedly unlocked and opened the door. As he stepped in, we greeted each other with a long embracing hug and kiss. He said, man I missed you. I replied, I missed you too. We begin to reminisce on the entire weekend when we conceived, speaking on future plans, ventures. We poured our feelings out to one another. He rubbed my stomach softly, while planting soft kisses. I can get used to this. I thought. I kissed him on his forehead, and we held each other for a little while longer. I was so comfortable with him. He had taken all of my worries away and I felt completely safe in his arms. I knew this was fate. I knew this was my magical story. I had once thought we weren't meant to be. But, this moment right here was proving me wrong. Our love was deeper than I thought. He leaned up and kissed me once more. He then said, I'm back with CICI. I don't know how I am going to tell her I have a baby on the way. And just that fast, my moment had been stolen. My heart had been shattered into a billion pieces. I looked at him and said OK. I was too hurt, to say much. Tell her when you are ready; just do right for your child with a smile. He said for real? I said of course, it's not anyone's business but ours. I could tell he felt lighter knowing I was willing to ride a secret out with him. Meanwhile, even though I was smiling, my heart had fallen out of my chest. Well, it's getting late King. I'm tired and I have to be up early. So, we can resume later. He said aight. He kissed me once more and left my apartment. What just happened? I thought. Am I dreaming? Did he love on me and then break hurtful news? This is the day the emotional roller coaster started.

Reflect: As I told Tough I was pregnant, he responded as if he was happy, then, he broke my heart by confessing he wanted to be in a relationship with CICI, and he was ok with keeping his child a secret.

(How did he respond? How did you feel?)

Chapter 15
Social Media Exposed My Reality

Fast forwarded….Ping, Ping, Ping, Ping. My notifications from social media were going off on my phone. I was extremely tired and now irritated that the phone was making so much noise. Nevertheless, the sounds woke me up. I grab the phone, got on social media and clicked on the notifications located at the top right corner. I discovered the notifications had come from people who were commenting on posts I had been a part of. I finally sit all the way, get out of bed and proceeded to use the bathroom. Shortly after, I grabbed a cheese stick and sausage from the kitchen, walked back into my bedroom and crawled into bed and continued scrolling through social media. As I was scrolling through social media, I came across a post with someone who mentioned my child's father name, nothing bad or alarming. But, it piqued my interest to click on his name to view the activity on his page. My grandmother always said, if you go looking for something you will find it.

There he was in a picture just as fine and good looking as he wants to be. But there was someone next to him. It was CICI. They were hugged up, sharing a kiss, and he was ramping and raving about her. I scrolled down more, he tagged her in a post with an engagement ring, scroll down once more, they had taken a trip to Vegas! The more I scrolled, the more I grew groaning pains in my stomach. I felt as if the walls were caving in on me and I was trapped in a deadly tunnel. I said aloud, who the f*** do he think he is. He come over here showed me love; and now he is publicly on social media representing CICI, taking trips, when I am pregnant with his child! He hasn't even offered to buy a pack of diapers. He has never accompanied me for a Dr's visit! He is acting as if I don't even exist! I was sad and furious at the same time. The only thing I could do in that moment is cry myself back to sleep.

The behavior he was displaying was odd, different, and also hurtful to me. I said to myself, I have dated Tough on and off for three years and we shared a very close mutual friend and several mutual friends on social media. All the while I had never heard or seen him mention CICI on his social media page. But, even though in reality, I could see the social media post back-to-back, my subconscious mind was telling me, it wouldn't last. I was really where he wanted to be. I continued to cry myself to sleep.

Later in the night around 9:00pm, Tough called and asked if he could come over to rub my stomach and his knee was hurting and he wanted a massage. My mind was telling me no, but my heart and my mouth was saying, "sure babe" come on. I then said, hey can you stop and grab me some food. He said aight Queen, I got you. I hung up the phone and let out a hard sigh. Here we go again, I thought. But, it didn't stop me from freshening up and putting on sexy night clothes. Some people would say, I was the perfect example for being stuck on stupid.

Tough finally arrived with food in his hands, lots of hugs and kisses. I was feeling excitement once more. I couldn't explain how he did it or what he did, it was simple he just did it for me. We sat on the couch and watched a little bit of TV; he rubbed my stomach and I gave him a massage as promised. Halfway through the visit, I asked him about his feelings. I wanted to know. Was I crazy for thinking he truly loved me or does he love me?

Tough?" Yes Queen. So, uhm I have a question and I need you to be honest. He said, "Ok" How do you feel about me and our baby? He said I love you. I'm not mad you are pregnant, or that is by you, it's just not good timing. He goes on to say, I am in love with two people, you and CICI. I think it would be best if you get an abortion, because I will not be able to be there for the baby, because I am in a relationship. I didn't say anything at the time. As a matter of fact, after he told me this, tears were rolling down my face. He leaned over and kissed me. You see, his kisses had a way of taking me from Earth to Mars. He gave me a tight hug and said don't cry, I am not trying to hurt you. I said, it's ok, I'm fine. I walked him to the door and he left.

He begin to text me as he was driving home and said, don't be mad but, I think we should get an abortion. I don't want to bring a baby into this world like this. I lost all my calm …. all my coo. He was already throwing Mike Tyson hits and I was taking them. But, now he was going for the KO like Muhammad Ali. I replied, "This is my first child, I will not get an abortion. If you choose not to be around that's on you. But, I will not kill my first child". At this instant, I began to sob softly. How can I do this? I will never be able to pull this off. A single parent, the father is already gone? How could the one I loved so much, said he loved me, what I thought was my dream come true, choose to desert us? How did my role, value change to him overnight? These were thoughts that started and never stopped. They became more frequent as time passed causing long dreary days and many sleepless nights.

As the days and weeks went by, communication between Tough and I had become less. Meanwhile there was an influx of social media posts on his page about CICI. It hurts me to see those posts, but I continued to seek the pain. Tough went from showing up regularly to periodically to when he wanted or needed something. But, just a little bit of him at that moment was pacifying me.

Chapter 16
He loves me He loves me not

Vivian Green, an R and B artist sang, Last night I cried, tossed and turned, woke up with dry eyes, my mind racing, feet were pacing, Lord, help me please, tell me what I have gotten into. I'm on an emotional rollercoaster, loving you aint nothing healthy, loving you was never good for me, but I can't get off this emotional rollercoaster. I played this song over and over and over again. This song describes exactly what I was feeling while being single, and pregnant by Tough. One minute he would show love, concern, and excitement, the next he acted as if I was a one night stand and he didn't even know my first name. There were times when we were intimately involved, he took his time and gave passion, other times it was a wham bam thank you ma'am. I was truly on an emotional rollercoaster and Tough was in control. He was so much in control; my dreams were even controlled. I remember this one instance; I would like to say it was a prophetic moment or emotionally and mentally trigger. But, I had a dream Tough had proposed to Cici and they were planning a wedding. But, there was still some distance as if it didn't quite happen. I found myself popping up out of my sleep, gasping for air, sick to my stomach that it was true, he was going to tie the knot and my unborn child and I would be left in the dust. I walked to the kitchen and poured a glass of water and stood against the counter with my head in my hands. Ebony. Get it together. It was just a dream. He will not marry her. Calm down. I looked to my left and saw my cellular phone on the counter charging. "How about I just call him and ask him if he is getting married. He'll tell the truth, I thought. I hadn't talked to him in a week or so, I was nervous, but I wanted to know. He answers the phone, hey Tough, hey what's up he replied. Are you getting married? He said I thought about it. I said to who Cici? He said yes. I feel like it's the right thing to ... Click. I hung up the phone. I needed to hear no more. The deal was sealed. I had to get off of this emotional rollercoaster.

Chapter 17
Begging for Mercy

Jesus, Jesus, Jesus, Jesus. Jesus. Jesus. Help. Jesus. Where are you? If you can hear me, can you listen to me? I know I have fallen short of your glory. I know I willingly and deliberately committed sin outside of your will. I know I hurt your feelings. I am sorry. Will you accept my apology? I know I haven't said much to you lately. But I have not forgotten your promise. Your words say: 1 John 1:9 if we confess our sins, you are faithful and just to forgive us our sins and to cleanse us from all unrighteousness.

I was in the middle of my bedroom floor holding my stomach, lying in fetal position, hoping and praying the King, My Father would hear me and accept my apology. This entire time, I was blaming him for my pain. I was blaming him for the turmoil and humiliation I was feeling. But, blaming was not helping. I realized he didn't do this. I did this. I was the reason I was on this emotional rollercoaster with Tough, and it was going full speed. Not only had I isolated myself from family and friends, I isolated myself from God. The pain I was experiencing was so excruciating. I was forced to go back to God, weeping for forgiveness and mercy. I closed my eyes and wept more. I could feel the warm tears caressing my face. As, I began to clutch my stomach tighter, the Holy Spirit, dropped a word of revelation. Psalm 103:10-14 – He has not punished us as we deserve for all our sins, for his mercy toward those who fear and honor him is as great as the height of the heavens above the earth. You are forgiven. Get up and wipe your tears my child. If I had to describe the voice I heard, I would describe it as a gentle, clear whisper. It was very smooth, still and calming. I wasn't familiar with this voice and it was just me in the room. Therefore, I was certain, my Father had heard me. I followed his instructions. I stood up and wiped my tears. I am standing here in silence. Now what?

Reflection:

Who are you blaming for your abandonment? Do you feel guilty? I encourage you to read and digest God's word on forgiveness and begin to feed your soul with his promise.

_____

_____

_____

_____

Chapter 18
That's Your Baby

Mama... Well, not my birth mother. My grandmother came to mind. I wasn't sure what my next step was. But I knew someone whom I loved dearly, trusted and whom I knew had my best interest at heart could potentially give me insight into my current circumstance. So, I followed my intuition, and I called my grandmother. My grandmother has been my backbone my entire life. My grandmother has always stood in the absence of my mother and father. She knew me better than I knew myself. My grandmother is a wise woman. She never sheltered my sisters and I. She would always give us the reality on all situations of life such as relationships, friendships, sex, heartbreak, you name it. There was not a topic she left uncovered. But it has been said, Mama can't prepare you for everything, some things are trial and error.

Hey Grandma, what are you doing? Aww …nothing, walking back and forth" she said. HAHAHAHA, I laughed. Grandma you are always doing something. We begin to have a conversation about my unborn baby and my fears, pains etc. that I was experiencing. She said girl, you been so quiet, I didn't know what was going on. I said, yeah, I know. I feel like it's no one else's problem, so I just try to keep my emotions and issues to myself. She said, "noo, you don't ever feel like you have to keep something from me, or you can't call and talk to me. I don't care if it's the same issue. I'm grandma and I will be here. She said, one thing I will tell you is this, that's your baby. The daddy can come and go at any time but you don't have that choice. So, you love that baby with everything in you and if the end result is just you and him, Oh well. That's Tough's lost. But you have me, and you have family."

I told my grandmother, "thank you." I don't know what I would ever do without you. You have truly changed my perspective. As we ended the call, I felt empowered to conquer and defeat this beast of abandonment and rejection. If I didn't or couldn't do it for myself, I had to do it for my son.

Reflect: Why is healing important for you? What would your life look like or how

would it change, if you were completely healed mentally and emotionally?

_____

_____

Chapter 19
I called him Jeremiah

I am now 18 weeks into my pregnancy. I am far enough along that I can pay for a 3D ultrasound to discover the sex of my unborn child. As I am driving to my appointment, I had the radio station tuned into 1310. Pastor J. Johnson was preaching from the Book of Jeremiah. He chose the Scripture 29:11: "For I know the plans I have for you to ---------". He goes on to say Jesus knows exactly where he wants you. Nothing is happening to you by mistake. Your trial didn't just sneak up on you; God has a plan to use it for your purpose. Say it Pastor J. Whooooo. Hmm. Yes Lord, Thank you Jesus. I praised God aloud. It was refreshing to hear, what I believed to be God speaking to me through Pastor Johnson. Jesus has a plan for me. I said to myself, if it is a boy, I will name him Jeremiah.

I arrived at the facility alone and nervous. I couldn't believe how quickly five months passed and how I was finding out the sex of my child alone. But I had come to grips in that instant once more, this was my reality. I lay on the bed and the Ultrasound tech pulled out some cold gel, and a piece of equipment that looks like a wand and she rubbed my stomach back and forth, up and down for like 10 mins. Uh oh, I see something. She started pressing buttons on her machine and zoomed in. I started holding my breath. In my head, I'm saying hurry up, move it in the right place so I can see. Aren't you an expert? She said, "it …it …it is a boy! Yess! I am so happy. I will be a boy mom. She helped me up from the table, made digital copies of my video and said congratulations! I realized I was chosen. God chose me to raise his son. What an honor! I drove off all smiles feeling blessed. Sadly, and selfishly, I had spent five months of my pregnancy caught in the web of abandonment that I failed to enjoy the blessing that was growing inside of me. I realized many people can't bear kids. But I was pregnant with a boy! Jeremiah will be his name. Hallelujah! God is good.

Reflect: Have you found that one thing that makes you smile or give you a warm and fuzzy feeling when you think about your pregnancy? Have you allowed God in enough to reveal to you, the joy you will experience with baby? If not, I challenge you to open your mouth and ask God to give you revelation.

_____

_____

_____

_____

Chapter 20
Deliverance through Forgiveness

As time progressed, the hope and desire of my child's father experiencing the pregnancy and birth of our unborn child turned into hopelessness. The proof was in the pudding. I had become a statistic that I had tried to avoid. I had the chance to break the generational curse of abandonment that I had experienced from my father, and here I was watching my son experience abandonment before he was born.

The talk with my grandmother and listening to Pastor Johnson sermon had inspired me.... in the moment. But, when I was alone again, I found myself reflecting on the pain once again. The idea and behaviors of isolation became second nature for me. My routine had become work, home, and sleep. The state of depression had taken a seat next to me and was enjoying the ride. Depression slowly turned into anger and rage. I often had the urge to unleash the beast inside of me and seek revenge. I had friends chattering in my ear, suggesting how they would slash his tires, bust his windows in his car, get him fired etc, pull up and fight. My friends would say let me know when you are ready, and we can cause havoc. Oh, how they would get me hype and, in that moment, I was ready to dress in all black and make a mess on any scene. But I knew my life would not be the only life affected. My unborn child's life would be greatly impacted. So, I began to do the only thing I knew how to do. The one thing I knew for sure that could knock down mountains, bring me peace, restoration, and favor. I fell to my knees again and prayed. This time I was looking for revelation, and instant healing. I heard a quiet voice whisper the scripture, "Deuteronomy 32:35, NIV, it is mine to avenge; I will repay, in due time their foot will slip, their day of disaster is near and their doom rushes upon them. God had given me comfort that I didn't have to move a muscle. He had everything under control.

After, I understood the abandonment of my child's father was not my battle and that God had us, I was able to redirect my energy on healing and preparing for my child's birth.

Chapter 21
Chasing after Healing

Healing can be defined as the process of making or becoming sound or healthy again. But, the question became, how do I begin to heal? I had allowed myself to dig this hole of pitifulness, shame, guilt, fear, rejection so deep that it seemed impossible to get out. But I knew I wanted out. I wanted to be free. I began to search every website and read every suggested book. But I didn't feel any deliverance. I once again, turned to my Heavenly Father. The only word I said was "HELP". Over the next few days, I listened to Gospel Music only, read the bible and Prayed daily. It was finally revealed to me that, in order to be set free, I must forgive the person who caused the heartache and pain.

Oh yes, God and I debated back and forth for a few minutes. I said, "in order for you to heal and deliver me, I have to forgive him first." One thing I learned about God on this journey is when he gives an order, he does not keep talking. So, I finally gave in and said ok I hear you, how do I forgive a person like him?

My mind was made up. My deliverance and healing was riding on my obedience. I prayed every day. I asked God to help lighten my heart, diminish any hard feelings. O 'Lord help me to abide by your word (Colossians 3:13) "Bear with each other and forgive one another if any of you has a grievance against someone, forgive as the

Lord has forgave you." Your word says" But, I tell you, love your enemies and pray for those who persecute you" (Matthew 5:44) O 'Lord help me to forgive and love my child's father even through his persecution against me. 2. I wrote letters to my child's father explaining how I felt, which allowed me to release anger and sadness. 3. I spoke life into my situation. I started writing and speaking affirmations and quoting daily scriptures became addictive. God's word became my medicine. When I knew what God said about me, I began to gain strength, confidence, and endurance. I would say I am healed. I am independent. I am loved. I am an awesome mother. I forgive my child's father. I praise you Lord, for you said I am fearfully and wonderfully made. (Psalms 139:14) and I believe it is so. I can do all things through Christ him who give me strength (Philippians 4:13).

I rinsed and repeated these three steps every day for 60 days. On the 61st day, chains were broken. I could see clearly. The black cloud that once hung over my head turned into blue skies. I could walk outside and enjoy the wind, fresh air, listen to the bird chirps without sadness, pains. The very most thing I thought was impossible became possible. I had been delivered. I could now enjoy the blessing that was given to me by heavenly father, my unborn baby. I realized he used my child's father as a vessel to create my unborn child. The real father, Jesus Christ, was there the whole time, he never left. So, being single and pregnant was no longer a death to my soul, my life, a repeat of abandonment. It became a celebration of a legend to be born. I was picked to receive this gift that no one could claim, but me! His name is Jeremiah. Jeremiah 1:5 says before I formed you in the womb, I knew you, before you were born, I set you apart.

Chapter 22
"I AM"

Deliverance, happiness, joy took over. I was no longer focused on what happened to me in the past. I remember asking God to use me how he saw fit. I didn't know pain was involved hahhaa.., I.E. be careful what you asked for. Nevertheless, I was near the end of my pregnancy and I was fearless. I accepted my situation and I have forgiven my child's father and myself. The weight of embarrassment, shame and what others thought of me, no longer mattered. I no longer saw myself as Tough's baby mama. I am evolving from the naïve, weak girl, who desperately needed Tough to validate me. I am becoming a woman of Strength named Ebony D, Jeremiah's Mother. Whoooo!! The power of PAIN and forgiveness! I not only forgive my child's father, I thank him daily for giving me one of many gifts. I was able to enjoy the remainder of my pregnancy and prepare for Jeremiah's birth. Thank You Jesus!

My abandoned pregnancy was and is a part of the plan. In the words of Patrice Washington, "It didn't happen to me, it happened for me." What I thought was my ending, was my beginning. A Prince "my son" would soon be born.

 Signed

Mommy Enthusiast

Ebony D.

Road to Recovery From An Abandoned Pregnancy Challenge

Bonus Challenge:

Congratulations! Mommy Friend! You have made a choice to Heal! I am so proud of you! The truth is my story is not your story. But, we have one thing in common, We Desire to Heal Mentally and Emotionally Permanently and become the best version of ourselves.

I want to invite you to complete the "Road to Recovery Challenge" so that you can start Recovering from An Abandoned Pregnancy.

To be successful for this challenge, you will need a journal, pen, paper and all of your pain.

The Purpose of Journaling, Meditation, Prayer

Journaling- Journaling provides privacy. You can be as real as you want; A journal will not judge you or give you bad advice. A journal will not spread your business, give you a bad name. Journaling is your FRIEND, CONFIDENT, SECRET KEEPER. Mommy Friend, the time is now to gain a new Best Friend.

P.S. Have some fun (give your journal a name).

Mediation: Meditation can be defined as a tool that is used to train your mind to become aware of feelings, thoughts, emotions, vibrations.

The purpose of meditation is to simply heighten the discernment of your emotions.

Prayer: It is through prayer one can connect with the Holy Father, confess sins, ask for forgiveness, gain healing and allows one to gain an intimate relationship with him. It is through prayer that we communicate with God to receive revelation for the purpose he has for our lives.

Road To Recovery Recover From An Abandoned Pregnancy

Welcome to day 1.

Today we will explore your situation, dig into the wounds of your circumstance, we will understand, know, and become one with your circumstance, by using my three A method,

Accept, Aware, Adapt along with Journaling and ending with my prayer.

1st day —Acceptance, – Free Style Journal Activity

Acceptance can be defined as a person merely coming into agreement with the reality of their situation. In short it basically saying to yourself: "I'm in this *situation*. I don't love it or like it. I don't think it's right or fair but it is what it is, and I can't do anything about the past, but I can take control of the present and future.

Why: The purpose of acceptance is to understand what your reality is, and acknowledging that the sooner I face it, I have a better chance of moving forward quicker and living a better life. It is not to view your circumstance as good or bad, but puts your reality in perspective. The first step to any recovery is to get out of denial.

Free Style Journal Activity-

As you begin Journaling, "write the affirmation, My Mistakes are not Failures. I Am A Winner. Before you start journaling

Activity--

What is your story?

Who plays a role in your story?

Why do you think this has happened?

Take a trip down memory lane, and write every detail that led up to the abandoned pregnancy?

Good, bad, ugly

List the pros and the cons?

List instances of cause and effect?

Caution- you may feel sad, angry, happy, rejected etc. but, let yourself feel those emotions, it is ok.

In result, you will gain the big picture of your reality, and gain a better understanding and perspective of your lesson.

1. Identify the positive, and make a bold decision to move forward, sustain a positive mindset
2. Become more peaceful with the circumstance

3. Heighten your judgment on how to handle future issues

After completing the journal assignment; Answer the question: What is your reality?

Assignment:

Complete the fill in assignment

I have accepted my reality is _____ The positive I see in my reality is_____ (we will use this to generate positive energy, high vibration and remind us it's not all bad). The negative to my reality is (use this to help us to make better decisions, and to say we do not want this to ever

play a part in my reality again. (What are the emotions tied to the negative and positive?)

Pay attention to your energy when you discover the positive and negatives. (Are you higher, or are you lower vibration?)

At this time you should have a clear understanding of your reality, positive and negative, cause and effect. If you do not like your reality completely....

A shift, different direction and actions, mindset will need to take place.

Day 2: Awareness: Knowledge or perception of a situation or fact: Dictionary.com

Emotional awareness: The ability to understand Feelings

Purpose of awareness- is to identify who and what we are or were, likes, dislikes, choice of friends, etc

Our Goal: Understand the reason and season for crossing paths with our child's father:

TRANSFORMATIONAL THOUGHT LEADER AND CHANGEMAKER SUNNY DAWN JOHNSTON

Relationships are here for a reason, or season, or a lifetime.

If a person is in your life for a reason: and it is usually to meet a need you have, and once that need is met, then before you know, the relationship has faded one way or other, which typically means their purpose was served.

Season- If a person is in your life for a season, it usually lasts a little bit longer, it is time for you to share, grow or learn. This person may bring an abundance of happiness and laughter in your life, but it has come to an end, because it was only for a season.

Journal Activity:

What attracted you to your child's Father? How did you both meet? What was the environment? What were you doing? What was he doing? Who were your friends or clique at that time? How did he make you feel when you saw him, talk to him? When it was new???? Did he meet any need or fill any void? Did he help you grow in any way or learn something new? How long were you dating, kicking it etc. before the abandoned pregnancy? Were you mentally and emotionally stable at this time?

Result: How aware are you then? Identify if he came into your life for a reason or a season. Identify his reason and/or his season.

Show Gratitude; Give thanks: Fill in the blank: I understand my child's father came into my life for both a reason and season. I thank God for loving me enough to meet my (need) desire.

Affirmation: In my new reality, I am emotionally aware, understanding and controlling my emotions come easy to me.

***Day 3:* You will begin day 3 with Meditation**

Why: It releases stored energy, blockage and allows you to connect with our heavenly Father freely.

Steps to begin meditation:

1. Find a comfortable, quiet place
2. Meditate when you are energized and not tired and sleepy
3. Choose a comfortable position i.e. lying down, sitting up with legs crossed Indian style, sitting on couch, chair or bed.
4. Take a deep breath in. Take a deep breath out (3 times).
5. Find a guide meditation on YouTube that you like.

Abide meditations are really good for this exercise). Simply navigate to Youtube, search guided meditations for healing.

6. Enjoy this process; connect with God and the universe. Do not rush through this

2: *Journal Activity:*

Grab your "Secret Keeper" and begin to write: Reflect on your experience, use the questions below to help.

What do you feel? How do you feel? What was your experience through meditation? Did you get a vision, message, and confirmation?

3. *Write, Say, Post Serenity Prayer:*

Serenity prayer... God, grant me the *serenity* to accept the things I cannot change, courage to change the things I can, and wisdom to know the difference. Father, give us the courage to change what must be altered, *serenity* to accept what cannot be helped, and the insight to know the one from the other.

(Repeat until you feel a shift). Release-- hear the goal is to break the emotional strongholds and subconscious mindset thinking that you will never overcome this pain. It is possible to release the negative emotions that have taken over our minds and hearts. We will let go of those emotions that keeps us running back and wanting our child's father.

Day 4: Navigate to the Facebook page: I Am Ebony D: Recovering From An Abandoned Pregnancy or access the link: https://www.facebook.com/groups/717958528973926

Connect with me and other Mommy Enthusiast's.

You will receive additional guidance, instruction, support and love to heal from an abandoned pregnancy.

Meet Ebony D.

Ebony D. Davis also known as the Mommy Enthusiast, has an undeniable love for serving others, empowering Mothers and performing the works of God.

She is a Single Mother to a boy Prince. Ebony D. Davis believes and brags that it is because of her son, the mercy and grace of Jesus Christ that she has stepped into her calling of mentoring single Mothers by telling her story.

Ebony is a Praise and Worship Dancer, Queen Squad Health and Wellness Coach, and Founder of Road to Recovery from an Abandoned Pregnancy.

Road to Recovery from an Abandoned Pregnancy is a phenomenal mentorship program that capitalizes on bringing mental and emotional healing to single Mothers who have or is experiencing an abandoned pregnancy. In this mentorship program Ebony D. utilizes the medicines of prayer, meditation, and journaling...

Ebony D. Davis is an upcoming author who tells her story through her first book. The Gift of Pain -Persevere Through an Abandoned Pregnancy... which launched November 28, 2020. Ebony represents "The Gift of Single Motherhood." through her clothing line JED Designz.

Ebony D. Davis can be described as being down to earth, warm, straight no chaser, love people openly and endlessly... She greets people with hugs, laughter, and a fun, unforgettable personality without a doubt.

Connect with Ebony on instagram @iamebonyd..

Gift of Pain Ebony D. Davis

www.ingramcontent.com/pod-product-compliance
Lightning Source LLC
Chambersburg PA
CBHW050911160426
43194CB00011B/2365